Never Too Old For Purpose

John Stanko

Never Too Old For Purpose
by John W. Stanko
Copyright ©2025 John W. Stanko

ISBN 978-1-63360-313-4

All rights reserved. This book is protected under the copyright laws of the United States of America. This book may not be copied or reprinted for com-mercial gain or profit.

Unless otherwise identified, Scripture quotations are taken from THE HOLY BIBLE: New International Version ©1978 by the New York International Bible Society, used by permission of Zondervan Bible Publishers. All rights reserved.

Scriptures marked NLT are taken from the Holy Bible, New Living Translation, copyright © 1996, 2004, 2015 by Tyndale House Foundation. Used by permission of Tyndale House Publishers, Inc., Carol Stream, Illinois 60188. All rights reserved.

Scriptures marked GNT are taken from the Good News Translation® (Today's English Version, Second Edition) Copyright © 1992 American Bible Society. All rights reserved.

Scriptures marked NASB are taken from the New American Standard Bible®, Copyright © 1960, 1971, 1977, 1995, 2020 by The Lockman Foundation. All rights reserved.

For Worldwide Distribution   Printed in the USA

Urban Press
P.O. Box 8881
Pittsburgh, PA 15221-0881
+1.412.646.2780
www.urbanpress.us

Contents

Study 1 Old Thoughts	1
Study 2 Run The Race	4
Study 3 Finish Well	8
Study 4 Wisdom Dispensers	12
Study 5 Old-Age Faith	15
Study 6 The Mother of Faith	18
Study 7 As Good as Dead	22
Study 8 Die in Faith	25
Study 9 Won't You Be My Neighbor?	28
Study 10 Serving the Young	32
Study 11 Run Your Race	35
Study 12 God's Good Pleasure	38
Study 13 Gray Hair	42
Study 14 Thrive or Jusst Survive?	46
Study 15 A Gift From God	49
Study 16 The Way You Should Go	53

Study 17
Depression   56

Study 18
Faith Reasoning   60

Study 19
Your Legacy   63

Study 20
To The End   66

Study 21
Share Your Wisdom   69

Study 22
Term Limits   72

Study 23
A Crown of Splendor   75

Study 24
Decide Now   79

Study 25
A Time to Die   82

Contact Info

Introduction

After I released my book *Never Too Young for Purpose*, I was at breakfast with a friend who said, "Make sure you write something about us older folks and our need not to retire but to stay focused and on purpose." And since I am 75 years old as I write, it seems fitting that I should follow my friend's advice and write a book about the flip side of "never too young," which is obviously "never too old."

Some modern cultures legislate when their citizens are to be considered "old," recommending or mandating that they retire at a certain age. Other cultures portray someone's latter years as a time to retire from jobs, which leads to some believing their retirement is an entitlement. I disagree with both positions. Purpose doesn't come with an expiration date or "do not use after such-and-such-a-date" label. For example, Pope John XXIII became pope at the age of seventy-six. Golda Meir became prime minister of Israel at seventy-one. George Bernard Shaw had a play produced when he was eighty-four.

When we consider role models from the Bible, we see that Moses was 80 when he began a new career for the remaining third of his life (and we'll look at Moses in the coming chapters). But it's Caleb, the man who spied out the land and returned to give a good faith report, who stands out as the best model for our latter years:

> "Now then, just as the Lord promised, he has kept me alive for forty-five years since the time he said this to Moses, while Israel moved about in the wilderness. So here I am today, eighty-five years old! I am still as strong today as the day Moses sent me out; I'm just as vigorous to go out to battle now as I was then. Now give me this hill country that the Lord promised me that day. You yourself heard then that the Anakites were there and their cities were large and fortified, but, the Lord helping me, I will drive them out just as he said" (Joshua 14:10-12).

Obviously, unless the Lord returns, none of us are getting out of here alive. We will all die but that doesn't mean we have to cooperate with the process! The Bible clearly defines death as an enemy and enemies are to be opposed and fought. The best way to fight your inevitable passing is to be involved in purposeful activities until you can't perform them any longer. Even then, you can create a legacy of purpose that can live on and impact people long after you're gone.

What is your idea of "getting old"? Is it sitting around your home binge watching old movies? If you think you're too old, then you'll fulfill your own thoughts and thus disqualify yourself from a life of purpose. **Where in Scripture does it mention the word** *retirement*? **Is your interpretation of your latter years shaped by cultural norms or from the Bible?** I want mine to be informed and inspired by the word of God, which is why I'm praying "Put me in, Coach!" as I begin my 75th year. I want to be a Caleb in my generation.

I have the experience, the education, the health, and the desire to continue to impact lives and help build God's kingdom—and certainly the need is present not just in my nation but in the world. I'm doing what I can now to touch people through my travels and social media. As I do, I'm creating a trail that will help people navigate their purpose quest even after I'm gone.

The format for this book is the same as

many of my other projects and the same as *Never Too Young for Purpose*. I will write a short chapter using principles and examples from the Bible to illustrate what I am saying. As is my custom, I will include questions in most of the chapters to help you apply and understand what you read. The questions will be in bold so they "jump out" at you and can't be missed. In this book, since I am officially among the "old," I will include more personal illustrations than in my other books.

Therefore, I invite you to join me now as together we examine the truth that my premise "never too old for purpose" is true so that you will know how to prepare for old age—or make the most of it if you've already arrived. May God speak to and direct us as we study and walk together.

    John W. Stanko
    Pittsburgh, PA
    July 2025

Study 1
Old Thoughts

In some of my purpose coaching sessions, I hear people say they are "old." They think they should be further along in their purpose than they are and thus are fearful they are running out of time. Now that I'm in my seventies, it's funny to hear someone in their forties or fifties tell me they're old. My usual response to them is, "Old? You're not old. I have pencils and socks older than you are!"

The problem I go on to address is their thinking, for they have what I call "old thoughts" and old thoughts will make you and keep you old, even when you're young. We see someone else in the Bible who also had a problem with old thoughts:

> Zechariah asked the angel, "How can I be sure of this? I am an old man and my wife is well along in years." The angel said to him, "I am Gabriel.

I stand in the presence of God, and I have been sent to speak to you and to tell you this good news. And now you will be silent and not able to speak until the day this happens, because you did not believe my words, which will come true at their appointed time" (Luke 1:18-20).

When Zechariah claimed he was too old, I can almost see the astonished look on Gabriel's face: "What do you mean you're too old? I just told you God's will for your life and you're telling me it can't be done? I'm shocked! Do you know who I am? Do you know who I represent?" It seems that the angel then took it upon himself to sentence Zechariah to nine months of silence to reconsider and repent of his old-thought mindset.

You don't have to be old to have old thoughts. My friends in their fifties who say they are old have old thoughts. You can be in your thirties and have thoughts of what it's like to be old. You think that when you're old, it means your health will fail. When you're old, you have less energy. When you're old, you lose your memory. When you're old, you gain weight. Those are old thoughts and if you foster and protect them, they will become a reality—while you're still young!

Zechariah had nine months to think about the folly of his assumptions and when his son was born, this is what happened:

> Then they made signs to his father, to find out what he would like to name the child. He asked for a writing tablet, and to everyone's astonishment he wrote, "His name is John." Immediately his mouth was opened and his tongue set free, and he began to speak, praising God (Luke 1:62-64).

Your later years are not meant to be spent sitting in front of a window or computer while you watch the world go by. You have a lifelong purpose and old thoughts won't help you fulfill it. And when like Zechariah you think or say, "I'm too old," you're ignoring and dishonoring what the angel later said to Mary, "For nothing will be impossible with God" (Luke 1:37). Your old age is just another chance for you to show forth the glory and majesty of God's power, but you won't be able to do that unless you clean out your attic full of old thoughts, right now while you're still young(er).

Study 2
Run the Race

When people ponder currents events and listen to some of the teaching on the end times that's out there, they often ask me, "Do you think the end near?" If you've ever asked me that, then you'll know my standard response is "Yes, for me it's closer than it's ever been." And it's closer for you too. None of us are getting out of here alive and unless the Lord returns, each of us is facing an end that is somewhere in our future—which could even be tomorrow. Paul also had to face this question and stark reality:

> As for me, my life has already been poured out as an offering to God. The time of my death is near. I have fought the good fight, I have finished the race, and I have remained faithful (2 Timothy 4:6-7).

Let's quickly look at what those verses have to say to us.

First, Paul saw that his life had been poured out as a "drink offering." A drink offering was to accompany some of the animal sacrifices and was usually wine. It was to be poured into the fire of the sacrifice and while there would be some remains of the sacrificed animal, the drink offering was gone in the hiss of liquid meeting up with a hot flame. That's how Paul saw his life, as having been poured out, with barely any visible traces of it left.

Second, Paul saw that his death was near. It doesn't sound like he was being morbid or wallowing in self-pity. He was simply facing the fact that his days were indeed numbered. As I write, I have lived more than 27,000 days. If I live another ten years, that means I would have about 3,650 days left! When I look at it like that, it means that my death, just like Paul's, is near. In fact, it could be sooner rather than later. That's why I don't want to spend those last days in frivolous activity, thinking the Church or the Lord or society owe me something while I sit and await my end.

But then Paul looked back on his drink offering of a life and stated, "I have fought the good fight, finished the race, remained faithful." For Paul to say that he finished the race, he had to know what his race was. If he fought the good fight, he had to know what and who he had been fighting. And to declare himself faithful, he had to have done what the fight and race required him to do to win. That indicates he knew his purpose and had poured out his life to fulfill it, and was at that point stepping back to reflect on the journey.

I'm inviting you to join me as we follow Paul's purposeful example. After Paul wrote those words in verses six and seven, he then added, "But the Lord stood with me and gave me strength so that I might preach the Good News in its entirety for all the Gentiles to hear. And he rescued me from certain death" (2 Timothy 4:17). Paul knew his purpose, which was to take the gospel to the Gentiles. He was facing opposition but saw that God was strengthening him and would preserve his life until he had reached the finish line. He still had work to do and urged Timothy to join him where he was as soon as possible.

Do you know your purpose? Are you fulfilling it? Are you content at this point in your life to be "poured out as a drink offering," perhaps less seen but still heard as you serve the needs of others? Are you assisting younger Timothys in their purpose work, providing the wisdom and perspective only age can produce?

I want to do a self-assessment like Paul and be accurate in saying, "Yes, I did what I was supposed to do. I was faithful. And now it's in God's hands." May God give you the grace and vitality in your latter years to say the same thing.

Study 3
Finish Well

In this third *Never Too Old for Purpose* lesson, we look at a man who seems like he was old at the time of the story reported in Luke 2:

> Now there was a man in Jerusalem called Simeon, who was righteous and devout. He was waiting for the consolation of Israel, and the Holy Spirit was on him. It had been revealed to him by the Holy Spirit that he would not die before he had seen the Lord's Messiah. Moved by the Spirit, he went into the temple courts. When the parents brought in the child Jesus to do for him what the custom of the Law required, Simeon took him in his arms and praised God, saying: "Sovereign Lord, as you have promised, you may now dismiss your servant in peace . . ." (Luke 2:25-29).

Let's take a look at some lessons from Simeon that can help you later in life as you serve the Lord through your purpose.

1. **You don't have to have a title for God to use you.** Simeon wasn't part of the priestly family but was simply identified as a man who was "righteous and devout." The Spirit revealed something to him that He did not reveal to those with an official title or Temple position.

2. **Being in touch with the Spirit is the key to ongoing effectiveness for the Lord.** The Holy Spirit is mentioned three times in three verses. Your old age is no guarantee of wisdom or spiritual insight but your relationship with the Holy Spirit is a guarantee that God can and will use you.

3. **You're never too old to obey.** The Spirit moved on Simeon to go into the temple courts. It doesn't seem he was told why he was going, he just went as he had many times before. This time his obedience was rewarded when he saw Jesus and His parents as the

fulfillment of the Spirit's promise.

4. **When you're old, you can serve to direct, encourage, and instruct the young.** Simeon went on to say that Jesus was the Messiah, that He was the way for the Gentiles to come to God, that Jesus' life would be controversial, and that His life would be a source of pain for Mary.

5. **Simeon finished well.** Simeon had not retired, but was interested in the things of God up to the end of his days. God used him in a special way that so impressed Luke that he included the story in his gospel account when the other writers did not.

Simeon was a happy old man because God had made a promise to him and to Israel. Then for whatever reason, the Spirit had chosen to show Simeon the fulfillment of that promise.

Are you ready to accept the role God has for you in your latter years even if you don't have an official title or role? Are you willing to help others understand their role in life by sharing your perspective and spiritual insight with them? Are you listening to the Spirit and what He

is doing even if you may not get to live long enough to see or enjoy it?

Simeon had not retired. Instead he was watching and waiting and was rewarded with good news. I urge you to follow in his steps and prepare for a life of significance that carries you through your last days so you can finish as well as you lived.

Study 4
Wisdom Dispensers

As we move on in our *Never Too Old for Purpose* theme, we see another messenger arrive after Simeon was finished speaking to Jesus' family in the Temple:

> There was also a prophet, Anna, the daughter of Penuel, of the tribe of Asher. She was very old; she had lived with her husband seven years after her marriage, and then was a widow until she was eighty-four. She never left the temple but worshiped night and day, fasting and praying. Coming up to them at that very moment, she gave thanks to God and spoke about the child to all who were looking forward to the redemption of Jerusalem (Luke 2:36-38).

Anna had been married for seven years when her husband died and was 84 when she met Jesus, so she had probably been a widow for more than sixty years. She was recognized as a prophet (so much for those who think women should not be allowed a ministry role) and was probably given living quarters in the Temple, which is why she was there "day and night."

So while Anna had a title and a place in the "church" of her day, few people were listening to her any longer. Yet she continued to faithfully do what she knew to do, and God was watching. While the priests and other officials had long ago disregarded her ministry, she went right to some of the "common people," namely Joseph and Mary, to share what God had shown her concerning their son. We aren't told if she was able to pass that information on to anyone else.

If you grow old in the Lord, you will accumulate wisdom from your experiences. Not everyone will want the wisdom you can dispense, but some will. And you should position yourself, as Anna did, to be able to share what you see and know with those who will listen. That means you will have to accept a diminished role in the eyes of some, but not in the eyes of God. How did Luke know about this story between Anna and Jesus? Undoubtedly Mary told him fifty years later when he interviewed her while writing his gospel account.

Are you willing to accept a smaller but still important role in God's master plan as you grow older? Are you willing to mentor and direct the young, those who are willing to listen? Can you be faithful to do what you know to do whether you have an audience or not?

As I write, I am 75 years old. I no longer have a role in a local church; those are now filled by younger people. But I write, consult, counsel, edit, and coach as God provides the opportunities all over the world. I'm working diligently to provide a legacy of material on social media and through my books that God can use now or after I'm gone in whatever way He chooses, which includes not using them at all. I invite you to join me as a wisdom dispenser to those who are willing and able to hear.

And one more thing: If you're young(er) and reading this, I hope you live a long life. But if you do, keep in mind that one day you will be where I am today. So take a moment every now and then to pay attention to what an older person has to say for one day you'll be looking for the same listening ears that we are hoping to find today.

Study 5
Old-Age Faith

There's an old proverb that says the old die and the young can die. That is the reality of life—and death. Unless the Lord returns, none of us are getting out of here alive. However, there was at least one man who found the secret of a smooth passing and that man's name was Enoch:

> By faith Enoch was taken from this life, so that he did not experience death: "He could not be found, because God had taken him away." For before he was taken, he was commended as one who pleased God. And without faith it is impossible to please God, because anyone who comes to him must believe that he exists and that he rewards those who earnestly seek him (Hebrews 11:5-6).

We're not exactly sure what happened to Enoch but it seems that he made his transition from life as Elijah had, who was taken up to heaven in a fiery chariot. But the point I want to focus on in this chapter is that the context for Enoch's life and death sets the stage for the Bible's most famous quote about faith: "without faith it is impossible to please God."

Whatever happened to Enoch occurred because he had faith in God, not just as a young person but throughout his life. His faith was what fueled his transition from this life to the next. His faith was the common denominator and expression between his now life and then life. I'm not insinuating that if you're older and have faith, you'll be like Enoch and somehow disappear without a trace. I am suggesting, however, that God sees your faith and will help you make your heavenly transition while living out your last days serving Him.

I've often said I would rather die in faith than live in presumption or fear. And therefore I have faith for things that may not happen until I'm gone—or may not happen at all— and I'm fine with that. I write in faith for a best-seller. I am trusting my work in Africa will outlive me. I live in faith for my children and grandchildren, niece and nephew. And yes, I have faith for the end of my days that I will glorify God up until the last, bearing fruit for the Kingdom and glorifying Him for the work He has done in my life.

Are you living in current-day faith or the faith you had as a young person? Where is your faith focus if you are older? (Where is it if you're younger?) Are you still being productive for Him? Can you describe your faith projects that you're trusting God in this life to do and see—or will die hoping for their eventual fruition?

Enoch was so consumed by faith that he graduated to glory without a ceremony. That's my goal too, that my faith will take me to the next stage of my existence where I will continue to serve God. I invite you to join me in that faith journey no matter where you are in your own span of life, for all of us, young and old, will only please God by living *and* dying in faith.

Study 6
The Mother of Faith

In the story of Abraham and Sarah, Abraham gets most of the attention for his faith, but he wasn't alone in his faith journey:

> And by faith even Sarah, who was past childbearing age, was enabled to bear children because she considered him faithful who had made the promise (Hebrews 11:11).

Another translation says it this way: "She believed that God would keep his promise" (NLT). Sarah was trusting God right along with Abraham and together they produced faith fruit that has been set forth as a model for all to follow down through the ages.

In this book, we're looking at people in the Bible who were fulfilling their purpose into their later years, which is why we have come to Sarah's story in this chapter. Sarah's faith journey wasn't perfect which means yours doesn't have to be either:

> "Where is your wife Sarah?" they asked him. "There, in the tent," he said. Then one of them said, "I will surely return to you about this time next year, and Sarah your wife will have a son." Now Sarah was listening at the entrance to the tent, which was behind him. Abraham and Sarah were already very old, and Sarah was past the age of childbearing. So Sarah laughed to herself as she thought, "After I am worn out and my lord is old, will I now have this pleasure?" Then the Lord said to Abraham, "Why did Sarah laugh and say, 'Will I really have a child, now that I am old?' Is anything too hard for the Lord? I will return to you at the appointed time next year, and Sarah will have a son." Sarah was afraid, so she lied and said, "I did not laugh." But he said, "Yes, you did laugh" (Genesis 18:9-15).

What do we learn about Sarah in this passage? At first, her thinking wasn't consistent with faith thinking. She was old and assumed that there were certain things she could not do at her age, and one of them was having a baby. She scoffed at such an idea, but then found out that God knew her thoughts and was ready to reveal them as a sign of His promise—not to condemn her but to reveal His power. Then Sarah lied, denying she had laughed at all, but God was revealing that He could not lie.

The beauty of the story is that none of Sarah's frailties, either physical or mental, disqualified her from receiving the promise or its fulfillment. Hebrews 11 doesn't focus on her weakness or doubt; it endorses her faith. And that's good news for you and me, for while God is intimately acquainted with our thoughts and actions, He's still willing to use us—as long as we allow our faith and not our doubt to have the last word.

About what have you said, "I'm too old"? Have you laughed at the thought of doing something for God that you wanted to do when you were young, but have disqualified yourself due to your age? And if you're young, do you have the thought that when you're old, you (and others) are pretty much impotent where purpose and serving God are concerned? If so, can you see that is wrong thinking?

If Abraham is the father of faith, I guess that makes Sarah the mother of it. Determine to follow both of their examples throughout your life which will ensure that you, like they did, will have lived a life of purposeful faith all the days God allows you to have.

Study 7
As Good As Dead

Hebrews 11 has a lot to say about Abraham, but let's focus on this one verse:

> And so from this one man [Abraham], and he as good as dead, came descendants as numerous as the stars in the sky and as countless as the sand on the seashore (Hebrews 11:12).

You probably know the story. Abraham and Sarah couldn't have children, tried to have one through a surrogate mother, and when they had all but given up in the natural, God moved and Sarah got pregnant. We tend to romanticize stories like this because the Bible covers the years in which they took place so quickly. But put yourself in Abraham's and Sarah's place.

They had to change diapers and walk with their sick child—in their old age. They had to cook and make a life for their child—in their old age. They had to train and teach Isaac the ways of life and the ways of the Lord—in their old age. Abraham had to take Isaac to the mountain to sacrifice—in his old age. I'm sure they had help but still, a child coming in their nineties was a major interruption of life as they had known it.

And now you are challenged to learn from and be like Abraham. That means you're to trust God to do something—your business, ministry, education, or provision. You're waiting, hoping, praying and preparing, but the fulfillment of your promise or dream is in God's hands. **So what if He doesn't "move" or act until you're at an age at which you thought, "it's too late"?**

I'm 75 years old as I write. I'll travel 100,000 miles this year. With God's help, I'll write five books and publish 20 more for others. I work six days a week, usually from 6 a.m. to 8 p.m. And there's no end in sight. I've prayed the prayer, "Put me in, Coach" and He has and is. Like Abraham, I'm past my prime but also like Abraham, I'm available to God so we can accomplish His purpose in and through me.

I'm not interested in retirement for as someone once said, "Why would I stop doing what I love to do nothing?" My latest doctor's visit gave me a thumbs up in every area, but I know that can change without notice. So even though, like Abraham, I'm "as good as dead" and in the latter part of my life, I'm alive in Christ to do all the things He puts before me to do

So what about you? What mindset do you have? Are you thinking "I'm as good as dead," and acting like it? Are you afraid to try something new or move into expressions of your creative purpose you haven't tried before because you think you're too old, afraid something "bad" will happen? Are you playing the "I'm too old" card, or thinking, "I'm forty and God has to move now or it will be too late?"

The truth is, it's never too late when you're in your purpose. You're only too old for purpose if you accept that thinking and then act it out. Or you can be like Abraham, seeing your best fruit in your later years, because you knew how to draw strength from the Lord as you walk in obedience to His will for your life, for which you are never too old.

Study 8
Die In Faith

In this chapter, let's backtrack and take a look at Abraham's great-grandson Joseph in our series titled *Never Too Old for Purpose*.

> It was by faith that Joseph, when he was about to die, said confidently that the people of Israel would leave Egypt. He even commanded them to take his bones with them when they left (Hebrews 11:22, NLT).

Joseph had heard the stories from Jacob, his father, that God was going to give the people the land according to the promise He made to Abraham. Joseph put his faith in that promise and was confident it would take place, even though Joseph himself had been in Egypt for 80 years when he was about to die. His people's population in Egypt by then was growing to the extent that it would seem almost impossible that they would be able to return one day to where they had buried Jacob, but Joseph believed it was going to happen.

What's more, Joseph left one command in his last will and testament and that was for the people to take his bones with them when they went back. That indicated Joseph didn't believe the return was going to happen any time soon, but it was going to happen and he wanted to be a part of it. It would happen almost four centuries after his death.

This makes me think of what Paul wrote in 2 Corinthians, quoting Psalm 116:10: "It is written: 'I believed; therefore I have spoken.' Since we have that same spirit of faith, we also believe and therefore speak." What did Joseph do in his old age? How could he fulfill his purpose to rule over his family as God had promised? He directed their faith focus to the promise of God that they would return to their home by speaking words of faith.

Then we read the report in Exodus that took place hundreds of years after Joseph's death: "Moses took the bones of Joseph with him because Joseph had made the Israelites swear an oath. He had said, 'God will surely come to your aid, and then you must carry my bones up with you from this place'" (Exodus 13:19). Joseph made a faith decision on his deathbed: "All these people were still living by faith when they died. They did not receive the things promised; they only saw them and welcomed them from a distance" (Hebrews 11:13).

He decided to die in faith, even though he did not receive what was promised. And I made the decision years ago I would rather die in faith than live in presumption or fear. I write now in faith that my books will outlive me. I'm building a publishing company that I hope will out-survive me. I'm teaching about what I believe the Church should look like as we move on in the 21st century. **What about you?**

As you grow older, what's your focus? The present or the future? The current mess or the future promise? Pessimism or optimism? Are you just living your life waiting to die or are you living to live, fueled by vibrant and active faith? Joseph spoke what he believed God would do. He was an example of the truth that no one is too old for purpose or faith living. Now it's up to you to come to the same conclusion and then live your life according to that truth, speaking words of faith until the day you can't speak any longer.

Study 9
Won't You Be My Neighbor?

Let's go back and look at a verse we mentioned in the last chapter when we looked at Joseph as a good example of someone who wasn't too old to flow in his purpose:

> All these people were still *living* by faith when they died. They did not receive the things promised; they only *saw* them and welcomed them from a distance, *admitting* that they were foreigners and strangers on earth. People who *say* such things show that they are looking for a country of their own. If they had been *thinking* of the country they had left, they would have had opportunity to return. Instead, they were *longing* for

a better country—a heavenly one. Therefore God is not ashamed to be called their God, for he has prepared a city for them (Hebrews 11:13-16, emphasis added).

The verse I want to focus on is "all these people were still living in faith when they died." Faith is a lifetime assignment. It's not an event, but a lifestyle. It's not a pill you swallow when needed but a spiritual vitamin you take every day. And faith isn't just for things you think you need that you don't know how you can get them, but it's to be applied to goals and aspirations of things God has laid on your heart to do.

In the passage above, we see what's involved in faith by the words in *bold*. First, we live in it. Our whole existence requires faith. When we drive over a bridge, we have faith it won't collapse. When we buy food, we have faith that it's not going to make us sick. When we go to the hospital, we trust that the people there are well-trained and competent. So to trust God for provision or to fulfill a promise isn't that unusual of a practice, since we're creatures who function best by faith—no matter our age.

People of faith also see things. They see the future so clearly, sometimes even the future after they have departed this life, that they welcome those pictures of what is yet to come and work to make them a reality for themselves and for those closest to them. I guess you can say these people are visionaries.

Then faith involves admitting the truth of who we are. Faith never requires us to deny reality. We just don't allow reality to have the final say. We choose to allow God's word to have the deciding vote. Abraham was as good as dead in age, but chose to believe God that he would have a son to serve as his heir. What's more, people of faith say things that are compatible with faith. For example, I never say "I'm too old for this or that." Yes, as I grow older there will be physical limitations, but I'm trusting God that my latter years will be as fruitful, perhaps more so, than my earlier ones.

After that, those with faith are thinkers. Faith is rational, perhaps the most rational act of our existence. Faith may involve our feelings, but at the end of the day, it requires that we weigh the evidence and the possibilities and allow faith to have the upper hand. And finally, people of faith are longing for something better, which is the reward of our faith. We have a destination in mind and faith fuels the journey. Now all this occurs regardless of your age. We're never too young or old for faith.

Having said that, how is faith impacting your life? Are you living or simply existing? Are you admitting the truth of

your own weakness but trusting in God's strength? Has faith affected your speech so that you are uttering faith words and not those of doubt and doom? And how about your thinking? Are you using your rational capabilities to concoct exciting faith scenarios or fear-filled options for your older life? And finally, are you longing for more—to do more, be more, see more, and understand more?

However you answered those questions, the final promise of this passage is for you: "God is not ashamed to be called their God, for he has prepared a city for them." I want to be a citizen of God's city and not just someone living on the outskirts of town because I was unable to take up residence in the place God has for me. I would love to have you as my neighbor there, but the price of admission is a life of faith up until the end. I hope you're willing to pay that price. If you are, I look forward to sharing faith stories with you as we talk across our backyard fence on Faith Street.

Study 10
Serving the Young

David lived to be 70 and at the end of his life had a problem staying warm. Let's read what his attendants did to address this problem:

> When King David was very old, he could not keep warm even when they put covers over him. So his attendants said to him, "Let us look for a young virgin to serve the king and take care of him. She can lie beside him so that our lord the king may keep warm." Then they searched throughout Israel for a beautiful young woman and found Abishag, a Shunammite, and brought her to the king. The woman was very beautiful; she took care of the king and waited

on him, but the king had no sexual relations with her (1 Kings 1:1-4).

There's nothing wrong with staying comfortable in one's advanced years. The problem in this case, however, was that while the servants were focused on David's well-being, one of his sons decided he wanted to be king. David almost lost everything he had worked for due to the insurrection of his renegade son.

> About that time David's son Adonijah, whose mother was Haggith, began boasting, "I will make myself king." So he provided himself with chariots and charioteers and recruited fifty men to run in front of him. Now his father, King David, had never disciplined him at any time, even by asking, "Why are you doing that?" Adonijah had been born next after Absalom, and he was very handsome (1 Kings 1:5-6).

The writer also lets us know that David created this problem with his son by not disciplining him "at any time." David's lack of fathering skills didn't just impact him or his family, but had implications for the entire realm. And at the end, it seems that it was more about David and his needs than the needs of the nation. What lessons are there in this story for us as we study the topic *Never Too Old for Purpose*?

It would seem the main lesson is that you never retire from God's Kingdom work or responsibilities. The same principles that got you through your life still apply when you're older. Certainly you should not ignore your physical limitations or needs, but they should not be the main focus for you or those around you. You must maintain a Kingdom mindset throughout your life, remembering that it's not about you or what you have done. It's always about Him and what He's doing and wants to do—even after you're gone. No one, including God, owes you anything for your life of service.

David was popular but on more than one occasion, his self-centered tendencies caused his subjects many problems. Determine to be a person of purpose right up to the end, not insisting your own needs be met but doing what you can to meet the needs of others. And don't look for a way for the young to serve you but find ways to serve them to ensure that they have a chance to be successful in their day just as you had in yours.

Study 11
Run Your Race

No one impacted the early church more than Paul—except for the Lord Jesus. In one of his last letters, Paul wrote Timothy to declare,

> For I am already being poured out like a drink offering, and the time for my departure is near. I have fought the good fight, I have finished the race, I have kept the faith. Now there is in store for me the crown of righteousness, which the Lord, the righteous Judge, will award to me on that day—and not only to me, but also to all who have longed for his appearing (2 Timothy 4:6-8).

Here are some thoughts to add to our study with the theme *Never Too Old for Purpose.*

1. Paul was being poured out

like a drink offering. The drink offering always accompanied another offering and was either poured on the ground or into a fire. Either way, not a trace of the drink offering was left. Paul saw that his life had been given to the Lord's service. He wasn't in charge of the pouring, but God was in control, determining where and how Paul's last days would be invested.

2. **Paul knew his end was near.** Paul had a sense that his departure was imminent. There was not a succession plan to follow for he did not have an official position to delegate. He had known and stated that he had completed his purpose—there was nothing left to do. And no one really could replace the unique calling he had lived and fulfilled.

3. **He had** *fought*, *finished*, **and** *kept*. As in other places, Paul used athletic references to indicate how he would describe his purpose journey. He had devoted his life to his God-assigned purpose. It wasn't a hobby and didn't take second place to a career. It was the main

act in his life drama and he had played his role to perfection.

4. **Paul knew there was a reward in store for him.** Paul had worked not for the Church or for the Church's leaders, but for God. He fully expected his reward to come from his "employer"—God Himself. He knew he wasn't unique or special in that regard, for anyone who "longed for [Jesus'] appearing" would receive the same reward.

Do you know what your purpose is? Are you fulfilling it? Is it a hobby or the main attraction in your life movie? Are you fighting for, running in, and preserving what God has given you to do? The beauty of Paul's life is the clarity he had of his mission and his absolute commitment to it that allowed him to run the race and finish the course. I urge you to be as focused and resolute as Paul was to that when your end is near, so you can be as matter-of-fact about your purpose race as he was—declaring yourself the winner by God's grace.

Study 12
God's Good Pleasure

Here is a one-sentence summary of Moses' condition at the time of his death:

> Moses was a hundred and twenty years old when he died; he was as strong as ever, and his eyesight was still good (Deuteronomy 34:7, GNT).

Because he was 120 years old, we may tend to dismiss his age as an aberration, an indication that people lived to be older "back then." But if that's the case, why would the Bible make sure we understood Moses' condition if it was so common then? Let's see if we can find out.

Of course, the most important reason is that God was with Moses and empowered and strengthened him. But what made Moses so special that God would preserve him for so long in the condition described? My bias leads me to conclude that Moses was a man of purpose and God was providing a lesson in the power that resides in living and not just dabbling in God's will for one's life.

Moses understood what his purpose was early in life: "Moses thought that his own people would realize that God was using him to rescue them, but they did not" (Acts 7:25). The people weren't ready to be rescued, however. What's more, God had more work to do in him, so Moses fled to Midian where he lived and worked for forty years (see Acts 7:23). Then we are told, "After forty years had passed, an angel appeared to Moses in the flames of a burning bush in the desert near Mount Sinai" (Acts 7:30). So Moses went back to Egypt to begin another 40 years of service until he died at the age of 120.

I'm not insinuating that when you find your purpose, you're guaranteed to live to 120 and will never need glasses. But I am saying that purpose is energizing and gives you a reason to get up in the morning and fill your days with more than mindless television or meaningless recreation. Purposeful people don't buy into the thinking that "I'm old and old people are frail, decrepit, and forgetful." To prove this point, let's look at a purpose hero of the church, John Wesley, founder of the Methodist church movement. Here is Wesley's entry in his diary on his 72nd birthday:

> This being my birthday, the first day of my seventy-second year, I was considering, How is this, that I find just the same strength as I did thirty years ago? That my sight is considerably better now and my nerves firmer than they were then? That I have none of the infirmities of old age and have lost several I had in my youth? The grand cause is the good pleasure of God, who doth whatsoever pleaseth him. The chief means are: 1) My constantly rising at four, for about fifty years; 2) My generally preaching at five in the morning, one of the most healthy exercises in the world; 3) My never traveling less, by sea or land, than four thousand five hundred miles in a year.

Now that's the summary of a person of purpose! **What is the "good pleasure of God" where your life is concerned? Are you fully involved in it or only dabbling? Is your focus your well-being or that of others? Have you bought into the thinking that old people are not meant to do much but wait around to die?**

God wanted us to know about Moses'

condition at his end so we could have faith that life is to be lived to the fullest no matter our age. Take a page from Moses' and Wesley's book and determine to be a person of purpose right up to the end, for the truth is, as we've learned in this lesson, you're never too old for purpose.

Study 13
Gray Hair

As we continue with our theme *Never Too Old for Purpose*, let me share some personal reflections on a passage from the psalms:

> I will always put my hope in you; I will praise you more and more. I will tell of your goodness; all day long I will speak of your salvation, though it is more than I can understand. I will go in the strength of the Lord God; I will proclaim your goodness, yours alone. You have taught me ever since I was young, and I still tell of your wonderful acts. Now that I am old and my hair is gray, do not abandon me, O God! Be with me while I proclaim your power and might to all generations to come (Psalm 71:14-18, NLT).

As I read this, I'm 75 years old and I'm trying to put myself in the psalmist's place. Here are some thoughts as I do:

1. **He declared that he will always hope in God.** As people get older, they realize that nothing else "works," at least that's my conclusion. God and His ways are the only reliable things in life.

2. **He promised to praise more.** I need less sleep and now often wake up in the night. When do, I spend some time praising and thanking God for simple things: health, provision, relationships, grandkids. I take nothing for granted and I go out of my way to praise and thank God.

3. **He said he would speak of God's salvation all day long.** I'm on social media all day, every day. As I receive something from the Lord, I share it as quickly as I can.

4. **He said he could not totally grasp what He was saying.** As I get older, I discover that the more I know, the more there is to know. Learning is a lifelong pursuit in the Lord.

5. **He went in God's strength.** As my physical strength wanes, I increasingly have to rely on God's strength on a daily basis. He has all I need.

6. **He promised to only declare God's goodness.** When you have lived long, you have more memories and they're not all good. It's easy to get bitter or cynical. I ask God to help me be neither, which means I have to be the opposite—gracious and trusting, childlike even.

7. **He asked for God's help until he was done proclaiming God's glory to the next generation.** My ministry time is increasingly invested in sharing with the young(er) about the lessons God has taught me. And of course, I write and publish so God has something, if He so chooses, to share from the wisdom He's given me with those coming after me.

The psalmist stated that he was "old and now gray." When I get a haircut and look on the ground, I wonder where all the gray hair came from until I remind myself that it came from me. I don't know how long I have, so I'm determined to make every day count, just like it seems the psalmist was determined to do.

But as I write, I realize that everything he wrote is as relevant and applicable to people of any age as it is for me. When you're older, your body reminds you every day that the clock is ticking toward the end. The good news is there's plenty of work to do, as the psalmist said, for those who are focused on doing it until they can't do it any longer.

Study 14
Thrive or Just Survive?

I ran across a few of God's promises to His older saints in my study for this book. The first is in Isaiah:

> "I am your God and will take care of you until you are old and your hair is gray. I made you and will care for you; I will give you help and rescue you" (Isaiah 46:4, GNT).

The second is in the book of psalms:

> The righteous will flourish like a palm tree, they will grow like a cedar of Lebanon; planted in the house of the Lord, they will flourish in the courts of our God. They will still bear fruit in old age, they will stay fresh and green, proclaiming, "The

Lord is upright; he is my Rock, and there is no wickedness in him" (Psalm 92:12-15).

Let's look at the magnificent promise in Isaiah. In it, God vows to take care of His people when they're old and gray. He also promised to "rescue" His older servants, which means that the old are not exempt from trials and tribulations, or from faith adventures that will require God's intervention and assistance. No matter what their age, God will still be their refuge and strength.

Then in Psalm 92, God promises that the righteous ones will still bear fruit in their old age, staying "fresh and green." In their later years, they will proclaim God's goodness. This doesn't sound anything like retirement or of being physically unable to perform good works or purposeful deeds.

We saw earlier in this series that "Moses was a hundred and twenty years old when he died, yet his eyes were not weak nor his strength gone" (Deuteronomy 34:7). It's not necessarily true that the old are also infirm. So if God promises to rescue the old and if they will still bear fruit, it also doesn't sound like they will retire to God's "home for the elderly." They still have purpose and God expects them to produce fruit consistent with their gifts and talents.

So what is your fruit? What is the

purpose of your life? You must answers those questions regardless of your age, for God's promises and expectations don't have an expiration date. What's more, since the joy of the Lord is your strength, if you want strength in your latter years, you must be doing the things you love to do, things that give you joy.

As I write, I'm 75 years old. I know I'm not getting out of here alive, but I don't plan on cooperating with the aging process. I want to thrive and not just survive. If the day comes I cannot write, then I'll dictate or draw or do something to declare that "the Lord is upright." I'll travel as long as I can and I'll broadcast the lessons God is teaching me until death prevents me from doing so.

By then, however, I will have left enough behind that, should God choose to use it, my voice will continue to be heard when my days on earth have come to an end. **How about you? How do you want to end? Do you want to just survive or do you choose to thrive?** Think about it and while you do, I trust you will be convinced that you are never too old for purpose.

Study 15
A Gift From God

When I was young(er), I read Ecclesiastes but it never made much sense to me. It seemed that the writer was a bitter old man who was disillusioned with life, love, and the Lord. For example, he wrote,

> God has laid a miserable fate upon us. I have seen everything done in this world, and I tell you, it is all useless. It is like chasing the wind. You can't straighten out what is crooked; you can't count things that aren't there. I told myself, "I have become a great man, far wiser than anyone who ruled Jerusalem before me. I know what wisdom and knowledge really are." I was determined to learn the

difference between knowledge and foolishness, wisdom and madness. But I found out that I might as well be chasing the wind. The wiser you are, the more worries you have; the more you know, the more it hurts (Ecclesiastes 1:13-18, GNT).

Now that I'm old(er), I read the same book and it makes more sense. The writer, probably Solomon, had experienced most of what being the king had to offer: fame, fortune, and the finer things of life. However, he came to the conclusion that it was all meaningless, vanity according to one translation. And then he ended his book with this rather depressing summary of old age:

> So remember your Creator while you are still young, before those dismal days and years come when you will say, "I don't enjoy life." That is when the light of the sun, the moon, and the stars will grow dim for you, and the rain clouds will never pass away. Then your arms, that have protected you, will tremble, and your legs, now strong, will grow weak. Your teeth will be too few to chew your food, and your eyes too dim to see clearly. Your ears will be deaf to the noise of the street. You will barely be able to hear the mill as it grinds or music as

it plays, but even the song of a bird will wake you from sleep. You will be afraid of high places, and walking will be dangerous. Your hair will turn white; you will hardly be able to drag yourself along, and all desire will be gone (Ecclesiastes 12:1-5, GNT).

But typical to this wisdom writer's style, buried in his lament on the futility of life, he gave us the answer to happiness and fulfillment. In the above passage, he advised, "So remember your Creator while you are still young" while earlier in the book he had written,

> This is what I have observed to be good: that it is appropriate for a person to eat, to drink and *to find satisfaction in their toilsome labor under the sun during the few days of life God has given them*—for this is their lot. Moreover, when God gives someone wealth and possessions, and the ability to enjoy them, to accept their lot and be happy in their toil—*this is a gift of God*. They seldom reflect on the days of their life, because God keeps them occupied with gladness of heart (Ecclesiastes 5:18-20, emphasis added).

So the key to a happy old age is to enjoy the Lord while you are young and do meaningful, purposeful while you can, remembering that life is short. When I was young, older folks always told me that my senior years would be here before I knew it—and they were right. Now I encourage you to make the most of the days you have, for they truly are a gift from God, and all of us are closer to our end today than we were yesterday, which is what Solomon was trying to tell us all along.

Study 16
The Way You Should Go

An oft-quoted proverb about raising children is found in this familiar verse:

> Train up a child in the way he should go, even when he grows older he will not abandon it (Proverbs 22:6).

Of course, first and foremost, it would seem that this training pertains to instruction concerning God's requirements for righteous living. But I think it's more than that. As we learned in my book, *Never Too Young for Purpose*, God is revealing to the young who they are and what He has created them to do. He was doing that for you in your early years.

But as we saw in that series, the concerns and difficulties of making a living can often derail or detour youthful purpose. But the good news in today's verse is that the instruction you received as a young person, whether about holiness or purpose, isn't as far away from you as you may think, no matter how old you are or how long since you have paid attention to it.

When I was young, I loved to collect stamps. I had a lot of U.S. stamps but the ones I really loved were the ones from other countries. I would research where those countries were located and promised myself, "I'll go there one day." Today I have been in more than 60 of those countries.

One of my rainy-day activities as a child was to play with my toy typewriter. I would type out articles from magazines or pages from a book and then stack the papers on my desk, pretending that I was writing a book. Today I have written more than 90 books and I'm still going strong. Now that I look back, I see that the "way I should go" was evident in those two activities.

And I was always a good student. I went back to school when I was 57 to earn my doctor of ministry degree. And now, at age 75, I am learning Spanish and just started Ukrainian in preparation for ongoing ministry there. Studying was always part of 'my way' and there's no reason to stop learning now.

So what was part of your "way you should go" when you were younger? How

can you reconnect with those things, regardless of your age? Are you thinking, 'I'm too old,' or are you thinking 'I can do all things through Christ and this is something I need and want to do'?

Your purpose and creativity don't have an expiration date and they are remarkably resilient and don't spoil or decay with time. Therefore, you're never too old for purpose thinking or purposeful action. I urge you to reflect on your past and find out what parts of it you can still bring into your present so you can have a purposeful future.

Study 17
Depression

After Elijah's victorious encounter with the prophets of Baal, Jezebel threatened to kill him in retaliation for putting her prophetic cohort to death:

> Elijah was afraid and fled for his life; he took his servant and went to Beersheba in Judah. Leaving the servant there, Elijah walked a whole day into the wilderness. He stopped and sat down in the shade of a tree and wished he would die. "It's too much, Lord," he prayed. "Take away my life; I might as well be dead!"
>
> He lay down under the tree and fell asleep. Suddenly an angel touched him and said, "Wake up and eat." He looked around and saw a loaf of bread and a jar of water near his

head. He ate and drank, and lay down again. The Lord's angel returned and woke him up a second time, saying, "Get up and eat, or the trip will be too much for you." Elijah got up, ate and drank, and the food gave him enough strength to walk forty days to Sinai, the holy mountain. There he went into a cave to spend the night (1 Kings 19:3-9, GNT).

By the sound of the account, it seems like Elijah was depressed, walking for an entire day in the wilderness and then doing nothing but sleeping and eating. God was with him, giving him rest and food, but God didn't allow Elijah to linger in the cave of depression for too long:

> "Return to the wilderness near Damascus, then enter the city and anoint Hazael as king of Syria; anoint Jehu son of Nimshi as king of Israel, and anoint Elisha son of Shaphat from Abel Meholah to succeed you as prophet" (1 Kings 19:15-16, GNT).

There was still work to do and God expected Elijah to carry on and also prepare for his eventual transition—thus he had to anoint his successor while he was still healing from his depression. Little did Elijah know, however, that God had a glorious departure planned for him: "Then suddenly a chariot of fire pulled by horses of fire came between them, and Elijah was taken up to heaven by a whirlwind" (2 Kings 2:11).

In this book, we have looked at various aspects of those who purposefully served the Lord in their latter years. We see in today's lesson that depression and fatigue are two of the obstacles that we all face no matter our age. However, when you're a bit older and have had a few more disappointments, the depression and hopelessness can become debilitating. Yes, the answer is rest and rejuvenation, but it's also continuing the purpose work God has assigned for you to do.

How are you doing these days? Are you tired and weary, fearful and disillusioned? Are you wishing that the end would come as Elijah stated to God? If so, God knows and He is with you. He will give you what you need to be healed and part of that healing is knowing that your job isn't finished—yet. Ask God to show you what's left for you to do and then slowly, as you're able, get back in the game like Elijah did.

It's true that every day your end is nearer than it's ever been but God has more purposeful days ahead for you. I can't promise that a chariot of fire is going to come and rescue you from your trials, but I can promise that God is with you and He is mindful of your labors for Him—and He knows how to reward His servants like you.

Study 18
Faith Reasoning

When I started this series, I wasn't sure how much material I would find to support the theme that we are never too old for purpose. However, there's been plenty so far with more to come. Let's take another look at Abraham in this chapter, specifically at the sacrifice of Isaac:

> By faith Abraham, when God tested him, offered Isaac as a sacrifice. He who had embraced the promises was about to sacrifice his one and only son, even though God had said to him, "It is through Isaac that your offspring will be reckoned." Abraham reasoned that God could even raise the dead, and so in a manner of speaking he did receive Isaac back from death (Hebrews 11:17-19, NASB).

Let's review what we know. God had promised Abraham an heir from whom would come a nation of people. After waiting many years, the heir finally came and they named him Isaac. However, when Isaac was about 15 years old (which made Abraham about 115), the Lord spoke to Abraham to go to a place God would show him and sacrifice the son of promise—Abraham's future hope.

Notice that it says God *tested* Abraham, which doesn't indicate Abraham was deficient in his faith, but that God was showing him, Isaac, and today's readers the depth and quality of that faith. Without hesitation, Abraham made plans to do so and would have sacrificed Isaac had not God intervened. What was going on here?

The writer of Hebrews tells us, "Abraham *reasoned* that God could even raise the dead." Abraham applied everything he knew about himself, his experiences, and his God to come to the conclusion that if he did indeed sacrifice Isaac, then God would raise him from the dead—an unprecedented action for anyone to consider in Abraham's day. We're told that in a sense, Abraham did receive Isaac 'back from the dead,' for in his mind and heart, he had already sacrificed him.

You can use the reasoning skills God gave you to find a way to do His will or to excuse yourself from doing it. What God expects of the old(er) is for them to lead the way in faith because their experience qualifies and equips them to do so. **What faith lessons of the past can you apply to the present in a way that will enhance and not hinder your progress in the Lord? How well are you leading the faith way in your family, church, or ministry? How can you do more to set a faith example for others to follow?**

After all Abraham had been through, God was still working in his life, even in his old age. And we're glad God did that, for we now have a sterling example of someone who was not too old for faith and purpose. Because he wasn't, we have no excuse not to walk out our faith even in our retirement years just as Abraham did.

Study 19
Your Legacy

The book of Genesis tells the story of one family and their journey from the land of Canaan to the land of promise, their story ending with them in Egypt. Of the three men—Abraham, Isaac, and Jacob—we learn more about Jacob than anyone else as we follow him from his birth to his death. Jacob left not only a legacy of land, which he distributed to his sons, but also left a legacy of words that blessed and directed his sons and grandsons. First he blessed Joseph's sons:

> Now Israel's eyes were failing because of old age, and he could hardly see. So Joseph brought his sons close to him, and his father kissed them and embraced them (Genesis 48:10).

Then he blessed Joseph:

> Then Israel said to Joseph, "I am

about to die, but God will be with you and take you back to the land of your fathers. And to you I give one more ridge of land than to your brothers, the ridge I took from the Amorites with my sword and my bow" (Genesis 48:21-23).

It's wonderful to leave a financial legacy for those coming after you, but it's even better to provide a spiritual one. Jacob or as God renamed him, Israel, did both. He left land (a bit more to his favorite son Joseph—he played favorites to the end) and then made a faith prediction that Joseph would return to the land of his fathers. We learn in the book of Joshua that the return occurred about 300 years later when Joseph's descendants buried his bones in this extra ridge of land that Jacob mentioned.

God used Jacob up to the very end so he is a good example of our theme, never too old for purpose. **Do you want God to do the same with you? What kind of legacy are you leaving for those who remain after you're gone? Do you have a clear testimony written or recorded as part of your last will and testament?**

Are you looking for opportunities to bless others in your latter days, especially encouraging them by sharing what you see to be their strengths and perhaps even their destiny in God's plan?

What more can you do to focus on the well-being and needs of others instead of your own as you enter the last segment of your life?

Often your own physical needs can increase as you age, but if you determine to be a blessing and to bless, you will be able to focus on being a blessing even while your energy wanes. Do what you can with what you have to leave at least a legacy of kind words and thoughts as you face your inevitable role of passing on your testimony and knowledge of God to those who can benefit from it after you're gone.

Study 20
To The End

We already looked at this story in Study 11, but let's look at it one more time from a different angle. When David grew old, we read this about his physical condition:

> Now King David was old in age; and they covered him with garments, but he could not keep warm. So his servants said to him, "Have them search for a young virgin for my lord the king, and have her attend the king and become his nurse; and have her lie on your chest, so that my lord the king may keep warm. So they searched for a beautiful girl throughout the territory of Israel, and found Abishag the Shunammite, and brought her to the king. The girl was very beautiful; and she became the king's nurse and served him, but the

king did not become intimate with her (1 Kings 1:1-4, NASB).

While David's staff was tending to his personal needs, one of David's sons tried to take over the kingdom:

> Now Adonijah the son of Haggith exalted himself, saying, "I will be king." So he prepared for himself chariots and horsemen, with fifty men to run before him. And his father had never rebuked him at any time by asking, "Why have you done so?" And he was also a very handsome man, and he was born after Absalom (1 Kings 1:5-6, NASB).

We know that David was lax in his paternal duties throughout his life. First, Absalom tried to snatch the kingdom by force and many people died in the battle resisting his efforts, including Absalom himself. Then Adonijah tried his hand at treason and was almost successful. What's my reason for sharing this story again?

This story reminds us that we all have purpose work to do right up to the end. Yes, your physical needs may change and require more attention as you age, but you still have a purpose to fulfill and things to create. And depending on your purpose, you may have matters pertaining to your legacy that require your attention.

Who will continue doing what you do after you're gone? Is your last will and testament complete? Have you said all that needs to be said to your family members? And what about recording or writing a short autobiography that includes the highlights and possible lowlights of your life?

The good news in this story is that Bathsheba and the prophet Nathan set a plan in motion to bring David to his senses so that Solomon and not Adonijah would be king. In the same way, it's never too late for you to set your affairs in order and make a difference in God's plan for things to happen while you're still here and after you're gone.

While you tend to ailments and conditions common to old age, don't ignore the things that God would have you do that only you can do. Make it your goal to make a difference right up to the end and leave something behind that God can use, if He so chooses, as a foundation and guiding light for those yet to come.

Study 21
Share Your Wisdom

There's an old adage that says, "respect your elders." I would agree but it's always best if an elder is respected not because of their past but because of their ongoing service to others. We read in Job that those up in years should have one important thing to give other people:

> Wisdom belongs to the aged, and understanding to the old (Job 12:12, NLT).

We need the wisdom and experience of those who have gone before us, but later in the book, a caution is issued concerning the old:

> "I am young and you are old, so I held back from telling you what I think. I thought, 'Those who are older should speak, for wisdom comes

with age.' But there is a spirit within people, the breath of the Almighty within them, that makes them intelligent. Sometimes the elders are not wise. Sometimes the aged do not understand justice" (Job 32:6-9, NLT).

Being advanced in years is no guarantee of wisdom and understanding, for there are young and old fools. **What's more, if someone has the wisdom and understanding, what are they doing with it? How can they make it available to others who need it? What are some ways to make one's wisdom available to those who need it?**

Teaching is one way, but not just face-to-face classes but also using technology and social media. But there's the problem, for many of those who are older are not in tune with technology while others are afraid of it and its implications. They don't want to lose their privacy. They don't wish to be "tied down" to using it regularly. They're afraid they won't do it properly and won't have enough energy or creativity to sustain their presence long term. Perhaps you share some of these concerns.

If social media is not an option, then what about writing? Can you start to develop your writing skills so that you have something to say and know how to communicate it? The most important point in all this is to accept that you do have wisdom to share but you must be passionate, desperate even, to share it. If you have that attitude, then you'll find ways to broadcast what you have, perhaps teaming up with a younger person who can keep you current on how to use technology while you provide the content. If you don't want to write, then find every teaching opportunity that you can.

So what's it going to be? Will you sit in a rocking chair, wishing that someone would respect your gray hair, or will you give them a reason to sit up and take notice that you have something to say? I know for me, I plan on being active and sharing my lessons that my gray hair has brought me. I invite you to join me in that venture, no matter your age.

Study 22
Term Limits

In Numbers 4, the Lord addressed the duties of the clans and families of the Levites. The Lord directed Moses to,

> "List all the men between the ages of thirty and fifty who are eligible to serve in the Tabernacle" (Numbers 4:3).

Notice that these men were to be between the ages of 30 and 50, not too young but not too old. As the duties of the tabernacle and eventually the Temple were better defined, we don't see that this age category for service was changed. It seems like Levites went into semi-retirement after the age of 50 and became elders who ruled by nature of their experience and the wisdom they hopefully developed through living a godly life.

I'm not writing this to suggest that 50 is

a hard-and-fast age at which someone should retire or step away from leadership or meaningful work. But I am writing to suggest that the Bible recognizes there comes a time when those who are older must acknowledge an important truth: They are old and won't live forever. They then must be *open and willing* to pass on the mantle of responsibility and authority at some point as they age.

No one owns their position, whether they work in a church or business. There's a season when they have energy and creativity to fulfill certain roles but when that energy and creativity wanes it must be recognized as happening. That can occur when someone is 50 or 60 or 70 but it will happen. And when it does, they must not allow fear to motivate them to hold onto something for selfish reasons. We saw this earlier in David's life when at the end, he almost didn't promote Solomon to his rightful place as king because he was focused on his own needs.

Are you open to the fact that one day your capabilities will diminish, and you may not be aware of it? Do you have someone who can tell you if and when that happens? Will you make it easy for people to take over for you, or will you hold on to the bitter end? Will you allow your feelings to be hurt when, for the good of your family or your organization

or your church, others decide it's time to change the role you have had?

The good news is that God isn't finished with you as you age. Allow Him to move you into new opportunities where your wisdom and experience are most needed and welcome. The Levites were still involved after 50; they just weren't carrying the heavy loads. Their season in ministry had term limits. As I write, I have a flourishing publishing business. I do relief work in Africa. I travel to speak and share my wisdom on life purpose I have gathered over the years.

I'm busy and happy, but I don't do what I once did as part of a church organization. I promise that God has the same for you, but you must face the fact that whatever you are doing or will do has term limits, and one day you will have to stop doing it. Make sure you cooperate with that day and don't oppose it by insisting that others honor your years of life. Accept your limitations and continue to serve the Lord in the ways you can.

Study 23
A Crown of Splendor

I'm going to finish this book the way I finished the previous one title *Never Too Young for Purpose*, and that is by focusing on the wisdom books of the Bible, of which Proverbs is a part. The book of Proverbs addresses many aspects of life, including finances, leadership, family, and business, and specifically contrasts the life of the wise and their antithesis, the fool. In this chapter, let's look at a verse that speaks to the young and not-so-young:

> The glory of the young is their strength, the gray hair of experience is the splendor of the old (Proverbs 20:29).

As I write, I've just returned from a missions trip to Kenya with a group of 15 of which I was the oldest member. At one point, we planted some trees at a building dedication and someone took a picture of me while I was bent over, capturing a view of the top of my head which I can't usually see in the mirror. When I saw the picture, I saw all gray, thinning hair. Another translation of Proverbs 20:29 says gray hair is a crown. If that's true, then I am sporting a pretty healthy crown right now.

The good news is we had some young members with us or as I like to refer to them, "young legs." They could run and jump and not get tired, whereas the older members who had made the trip before provided the guidance for their youthful energy. We made a good team not only because of our diverse gifts but our diverse ages.

It can be difficult for the old to admit that they have lost a step, both physically and mentally. We can't do what we used to do—or at least I can't—so we should stop trying and instead give younger team and family members with more strength the chance to excel. I see this in ministry where my aging colleagues continue to serve, convinced they've still "got it" when they don't.

Some continue on to collect a paycheck, using up ministry resources that could and should be used for other activities. People love and respect these leaders, however, so there's no one with the courage or heart to tell them it's time not to retire necessarily but to transition to a different role. And what role would that be?

It's the role of the advisor, the coach, the mentor. It's the role not of the quarterback or the captain, but the role of one who comes alongside others to provide a voice of reason and experience—the coach. And what if the organization someone with gray hair is in isn't interested in their wisdom and experience? Then it's time for the gray-haired one to find a way to share what they have to a new audience in a different organization or through social media or writing.

In 2014, I left a position in a church where I was well paid making a positive contribution. I was 64 years old, but I felt it was time for someone younger to gain the experience I already had. It wasn't about keeping my salary (and the church paid their pastors well) or hanging on until I couldn't function any longer. It was all about stepping aside and allowing someone younger with more "strength" to get the experience. Now I travel, teach, write, and publish. I keep busy and had a chance on this last missions trip to share my wisdom in Africa with people who were eager to hear it.

Do you have a crown of splendor, or in other words, is your hair gray, representing many years of life? If so, are

you ready to accept a new role, making way for the young? Or perhaps you are still young working with those who are older? Then you should keep in mind that you need the wisdom of the aged while accepting that your "young legs" will be the ones to run the race while your elders cheer you on. And of course, you're taking one step closer every day to the time when you will have your own crown of splendor.

As you read this, know that your crown of gray hair is on its way, if it's not already here. Whenever it comes, know that it's time for you to graciously accept the role that age gives you, which is cheering the runners on. The young and old can make an effective team, but only if the old don't pretend that they're young when they're not and the young don't pretend to have the wisdom that only years of life can provide.

Study 24
Decide Now

As we finish this book with the theme *Never Too Old for Purpose*, let's look at the words of Jeremiah, the prophet who God sent to His people with a word that would be ignored to their doom:

> "He has made my skin and my flesh grow old and has broken my bones. He has besieged me and surrounded me with bitterness and hardship. He has made me dwell in darkness like those long dead" (Lamentations 3:4-6).

As Jeremiah looked back over the years, the verses above were his summary of his condition which seemed bleak and depressing. He further wrote,

> "I remember my affliction and my wandering, the bitterness and the

gall. I well remember them, and my soul is downcast within me. Yet this I call to mind and therefore I have hope" (Lamentations 3:19-21).

As I write, I'm sitting in a hospital room with an elderly relative and this would perhaps be their testimony as well. They are suffering physically after the end of a long, painful life, The problem for this person, however, is that they can't finish the story as Jeremiah did, for after all was said and done, Jeremiah offered this conclusion:

> "Because of the Lord's great love we are not consumed, for his compassions never fail. They are new every morning; great is your faithfulness. I say to myself, 'The Lord is my portion; therefore I will wait for him'" (Lamentations 3:22-24).

As you grow older, you can easily have quite a collection of disappointments, failures, mistakes, and painful memories. You will then have two options of how to assess a life that perhaps fell short of your expectations. You can either be resentful, angry, or disillusioned, or you can take the position that Jeremiah took. You can trust and have hope in the Lord to the end, even if that end is bitter.

We can now thank God for Jeremiah, for his testimony and faithfulness have been an encouragement to God followers for more than several millennia. God put him through a lot, but he emerged victorious not for his contemporaries' sake but for ours. The time to decide how you will die is while you are still living, while you have energy and mental clarity. You can decide to be a person of purpose to the end, even if God uses you as an example for others in your latter days.

How and when will you die? No one knows the specifics but we can decide the conditions where we are at right now. **Will you be a person of purpose to the end?** That you can decide. I invite you to join me in that pursuit as we seek to honor God with *all* our days, both the ones with youthful vigor and the ones with diminished capacity. When we decide to do that, we will certainly prove that no one is ever too old for purpose, too old for God to use them as He sees fit.

Study 25
A Time to Die

When I was younger, I would read Solomon's words in Ecclesiastes and think he had a fatalistic and pessimistic view of life. Now that I'm older, my perspective has changed—on life, death, and his words. How so, you may ask? For the answer, let's look at another one of Solomon's conclusions for one last lesson in our *Never Too Old For Purpose* series. I hope you'll see, as I have, just how wise he really was:

> There is a time for everything, and a season for every activity under the heavens: a time to be born and a time to die, a time to plant and a time to uproot, a time to kill and a time to heal, a time to tear down and a time to build (Ecclesiastes 3:1-4).

None of us are getting out of here alive. What's more, while we're here, we're going to experience tears, setbacks, and failures, which we dread, as well as the things we love, like family, work we enjoy, and simple pleasures such as nature and food. While it's important to determine how we will live, it's also necessary to determine how we will die. No, I don't mean the way we will die, but the attitude we will have toward it.

As I finish, I'm still sitting with an elderly relative. I'm watching this person process their current situation and they have questioned why God would allow this to happen to them. I'm not judging this person, for I ask myself, *How would I face and react to what they are going through? Can I decide now how I will do that?* I've determined so far that I'm a teacher and I've spent most of my time teaching people how to live. Now I must teach people and those closest to me how to die, and much of that involves a mindset that faces the reality of their and my mortality. Solomon wrote,

> I also said to myself, "As for humans, God tests them so that they may see that they are like the animals. Surely the fate of human beings is like that of the animals; the same fate awaits them both: As one dies, so dies the other. All have the same breath; humans have no advantage over animals. Everything is meaningless. All go to the same place; all come from dust,

and to dust all return. Who knows if the human spirit rises upward and if the spirit of the animal goes down into the earth?" (Ecclesiastes 3:18-21).

Notice that Solomon "said to myself." That meant he was evaluating what he saw and was turning it into a life-and-death philosophy that would be of benefit to others. What was his conclusion?

"So I saw that there is nothing better for a person than to enjoy their work, because that is their lot. For who can bring them to see what will happen after them?" (Ecclesiastes 3:22).

Do you enjoy your work? Are you preparing for your inevitable end? How are you doing that? Are you giving thought to how you will die? I pray you have many years left on earth, that this season of life is a time to live for you and those closest to you. But eventually, you will have to face the fact that there is a time to die. There's no better way to prepare for that day than to leave a legacy of joyous purpose work produced with an eye toward eternity. Doing that will equip you with the life philosophy that has been the theme of this series, which is that you will never be too old for purpose.

Let's close with the words of the psalmist in Psalm 37:25-29:

"I have been young, and now am old;
yet I have not seen the righteous forsaken
or his children begging bread.
He is ever giving liberally and lending,
and his children become a blessing.
Depart from evil, and do good;
so shall you abide forever.
For the Lord loves justice;
he will not forsake his saints.
The righteous shall be preserved for ever,
but the children of the wicked shall be cut off.
The righteous shall possess the land,
and dwell upon it forever."

Amen. God bless you as you serve Him no matter how old or young you are!

How To Follow John W. Stanko

The Monday Memo
Every Sunday since 2001 I have written a *Monday Memo* to discuss topics like purpose, creativity, and faith. You can access it at: http://www.stankomondaymemo.com

The Stanko Bible Study
I have completed a verse-by-verse commentary on the New Testament and I am not writing a weekly entry in the Purpose Study Bible that examines the topics of purpose, creativity, goal setting, time management, and faith as they are found in the Old Testament. All these studies for both the Old and New Testaments can be found at http://www.stankobiblestudy.com.

All My Books
Are available for purchase on Amazon or through the Urban Press website
http://www.urbanpress.us

My Free Mobile App

You can download the PurposeQuest app from https://subsplash.com/purposequestinternationa/app
I have many hours of video and audio teaching there.

My Website

http://www.purposequest.com
has all my video and audio teachings, plus some print material, but doesn't have the daily devotional.

Social Media

I publish daily material on all my social media outlets: Facebook, Instagram, Twitter, LinkedIn, TikTok, and YouTube. You can easily find and follow me on any of those outlets by using my first and last name.

And of course, I am always available through my email address: johnstanko@gmail.com

Additional Titles by John W. Stanko

A Daily Dose of Proverbs
A Daily Taste of Proverbs
Changing the Way We Do Church
I Wrote This Book on Purpose
Life Is A Gold Mine: Can You Dig It?
Strictly Business
The Faith Files, Volume 1
The Faith Files, Volume 2
The Faith Files, Volume 3
The Leadership Walk
The Price of Leadership
Unlocking the Power of Your Creativity
Unlocking the Power of Your Productivity
Unlocking the Power of Your Purpose
Unlocking the Power of You
What Would Jesus Ask You Today?
Your Life Matters

Live the Word Commentary: Matthew
Live the Word Commentary: Mark
Live the Word Commentary: Luke
Live the Word Commentary: John
Live the Word Commentary: Acts
Live the Word Commentary: Romans
Live the Word Commentary: 1 & 2 Corinthians
Live the Word Commentary: Galatians, Ephesians, Philippians, Colossians, Philemon
Live the Word Commentary: 1 & 2 Thessalonians, 1 & 2 Timothy, and Titus
Live the Word Commentary: Hebrews
Live the Word Commentary: Revelation

Ediciones en Español
Cambiando la Manera de Hacer Iglesia

La Vida Es Una Mina De Oro: Te Atreves A Cavarla?

No Leas Estes Libro: (A Menos Que Quieras Convertirte E Un Mejor Líder)

Fuero lo Viejo, Adentro lo Nuevo

Gemas de Propósito

Ven a Adorarlo: Preparándonos para Emmanuel